Beginner's Guide to the Stock Market

How to Successfully Invest in the Stock Market and Start Generating Your First Earnings

David C. Russell

Table of Contents

INTRODUCTION

Congratulations on purchasing *Beginner's Guide to the Stock Market, and* thank you for doing so. My goal with this book is to simplify how the stock market works and how anyone can get involved. When most people think about the stock market, they envision a bunch of Wall Street millionaires and billionaires who practically live on another planet. They think of people like Warren Buffett or Charles Schwab and believe they will never reach these individuals' heights.

I have got some news for you. Many of the high-level investors in the stock market had to start somewhere. Yes, some had an advantage due to capital or knowing the right people, but others had to start at the bottom and learn from the beginning. If you are at this point in life, I am here to help by teaching you the stock market fundamentals. It may not be as difficult as you think. With the many advancements in technology and access to investing, getting into the stock market has never been simpler. It will continue to get easier as time goes by.

The following chapters will discuss exactly what the stock market is, how it functions on a daily basis, the history behind it, and how you can get involved right away. The stock market can be intimidating if you are not familiar with it, so starting with the basics is a great first step. From here, you can continue to learn more, which I always recommend. After getting into the fundamentals, I will detail more specific topics regarding the stock market, including the risk that it entails.

In the end, the stock market is not a game of chance, and no matter how familiar you are with it, there will always be risk involved. However, with extra education, training, and insight, we can all mitigate this risk, just like with anything else. A major section of this book will be discussing the volatility of stocks and what makes them rise and fall. This will give you more predictors of a stock doing well or not.

Learning from others is one of the best educations you can receive. Therefore, I will also go over some common mistakes that beginners make. As well, I will go over some of the methods used by the best minds in the business, including Warren Buffett. In addition, having control over your emotions will serve you greatly as you experience the ups and downs of the stock market, and there will be plenty. All of this knowledge will serve you well in reducing your risk. In the end, it is your money that is being used, so I want you to get the best return on investment possible.

As we go through the remaining chapters of this book, you will learn how to start buying your first stocks and which platforms are the best to use. You will be able to start trading like the best and start making money in the stock market in many different ways. You will be amazed at how anyone can use the stock market to increase their financial wealth. There are millions of people out there already involved and doing well in the stock market, so there is no reason you can't join them.

Finally, I will also get into more specific topics, like trading value stocks. Overall, my hope is that you feel comfortable getting started in the stock market and begin your investment journey to being improving your wealth. With the unpredictability of the job market, social security, and other safety nets we enjoyed in the past, having knowledge of investing is essential for continued success in your financial future. Even if you choose not to make stock market investing a career, you can still earn a healthy side income to save up for retirement or other interests you might have.

Thanks again for choosing this book; once completed, please make sure to leave a short review on amazon if you enjoy what I have to say. I'd really love to hear your feedback.

New York: The Financial Capital of the World!

CHAPTER 1: STOCK MARKET FUNDAMENTALS

Where do you go when you have run out of items in your fridge? How about when you need new furniture or tools? Each of these products requires us to go shopping at a specific location or store. Now, apply this same concept to the stock market. It is called a market for a reason, as we use it to buy stocks that we are interested in buying as an investment.

The stock market operates similar to an auction house, where buyers and sellers are able to negotiate prices and make the necessary trades. The market works through networks of exchanges, like the New York Stock Exchange or Nasdaq. Publicly-traded companies will list shares of their stocks on these various exchanges for investors to purchase. Investors can continue trading these stocks among themselves, and the particular exchange tracks the supply and demand of each stock listed. The supply and demand will eventually determine the value of each stock.

The two largest stock exchanges, which I mentioned above, are worth trillions of dollars when you add up all of their shares. With the volatility of the market, the exact value changes regularly. In fact, the market can be worth something completely different compared to the start and completion of a day. While the two biggest exchanges exist in the United States, other major cities, like Tokyo, London, Hong Kong, and Shanghai, all have their own major exchanges, as well.

While each exchange will match buyers to sellers, they all work a little bit differently. For example, buyers and sellers trade with one another, and the exchange matches the highest bid for the lowest sales price. With the Nasdaq, trading is done through a dealer electronically. When an investor buys a stock, they can hold onto it with the hope that the particular share price goes, resulting in a return on the investment. From here, the buyer can choose to hold, sell, or even buy more shares.

While the stock market hours vary depending on the location, they are mostly open around regular business hours. Therefore, trading is not usually done during off-hours. This was a rough overview of how the stock market works, and I will now get into more detail about specific topics.

What Is a Stock?

A stock, which is also known as an equity, is a type of security that represents partial ownership of a company. Therefore, if you buy stocks, then you own a fraction of that particular company. The more stocks you own, the more ownership and influence you will have. For example, an investor who owns

100 stocks of Nike will have greater ownership than someone who owns 50. Owning this equity entitles an investor to share in the profits. Each unit of stock is known as a share.

While the majority of stocks are sold through some type of exchange, they can be acquired through private shares, as well. These are allowed, as long as they follow specific government regulations. Whether you are buying or selling, make sure to understand what specific regulations your country has.

The reason corporations issue stocks is to raise funds to operate and eventually grow their enterprise. The shareholders now become partial owners and can influence certain decisions in determining what direction the company goes. The stockholders do not actually own corporations. The corporations stand alone as a legal entity, and ultimately, do all of their business dealings under the corporation's umbrella, including borrowing money, owning property, and filing taxes. Corporations can also be sued because they are their own asset. This fact greatly reduces the liability of the shareholders. For instance, if an organization goes bankrupt, the shareholders' personal assets will not be at risk.

It is incorrect for a shareholder to assert that they own a certain percentage of a company based on the number of stocks they have. It is better to say that you own the percentage of shares. For example, if a company has 1,000 shares, and you own 330, it is safe to say you own 33% of the company's shares. A shareholder cannot just do as they please with a corporation because the corporation still has control over everything that goes on. Owning stocks simply gives you the power to vote at shareholder meetings, benefit from dividends or company profits, and sell your shares to someone else. Being able to vote during meetings is where your influence comes into play. If you own a majority of the shares, your voting power increases, and you can indirectly control which direction the company moves towards.

Common vs. Preferred Stocks

There are two main types of stocks: common and preferred. Common stocks are the ones that give ownership stake in a company to its holders, and many companies exclusively issue these types of securities. The various stock exchanges have a lot more common stocks than preferred stocks.

The type of stocks I described above, where shareholders have influence over corporate decisions, are common stocks. The most attractive feature they carry is that their value can rise dramatically as the company becomes more profitable. Investors benefit greatly from this profitability. Of course, investors will also have to deal with losses in the event that share prices drop. I will get into the risks of playing the stock market more in the next chapter. For now, realize that it's not all fun and games.

Common stockholders are also the last in line to gain anything in the event a company goes under. First in line are lenders, suppliers, debt holders, and preferred stockholders. This is another setback these types of equities come with. Be aware of this anytime you want to engage in common stocks.

Speaking of preferred stockholders, this type of securities come with their own benefits and setbacks, as well. These types of stocks work more like a bond. The dividends for preferred stocks are generally higher and fixed at a certain rate. The redemptions price for these stocks are also set at a certain value, so investors are much more limited on profits. Basically, these securities offer lower risk but don't have the same potential for growth that common stocks do. Of course, receiving payment prior to common stockholders getting their dividends is another major advantage.

There are disadvantages to preferred stocks, as well. First of all, investors do not have voting rights and cannot influence the direction of a company. Second, there is limited potential for capital gains.

Both common and preferred stock options can be good; it just depends on how much risk you are willing to take.

What Is a Bond?

Stocks and bonds are two of the main securities you will hear about when you start investing. A bond is a fixed-income tool, which is basically a loan made by an investor to a borrower. Bonds are used by companies, states, or governments to help finance projects and various operations. For example, governments can use bonds to fix roads or infrastructure, provide funding for schools, or build new dams. Similarly, companies can use bonds to buy new equipment or perform new types of research. Owners of bonds are known as debtholders.

Bonds do not provide any ownership rights to an investor, unlike a common stock. As a result, you will not necessarily benefit from a company's growth. A bond is known as a fixed-security investment, and investors will earn a return based on the interest on the loan. In summary, when you buy a bond, you are loaning money to an entity and then getting the amount you loaned, plus interest, back to you. Bonds provide less volatility than stocks but also have less potential for high returns. Basically, they are a low-risk guaranteed investment.

What Are Options?

Stock options give investors a right to buy or sell stocks at an agreed upon date and price. There is no obligation for an investor to do this, which is why it's called an option. There are two types of options:

- Calls: These are bets that a stock will rise.
- Puts: These are bets that a stock will fall.

The expiration date of an option is important because it helps traders to price the value of a put and call. This is known as the time value, which is used in various option pricing models.

The strike price is what the underlying asset is to be bought or sold at when the option is actually exercised. Basically, it is the price that a trader expects to be either above or below by the expiration date. For example, a trader might expect a company's stock to be above $150 by the middle of March. They can then buy a March $150 call.

In options' trading, contracts represent the number of options a trader may be willing to buy. One contract equals 100 shares of the underlying stock. Using the example of $150, if a trader buys five call contracts, they will own five March $150 calls. If the stock rises above $150 by the expiration date, the trader can either exercise their option or buy 500 shares of the company's stock. On the other hand, if the stock is worth less than $150 by the expiration date, the option will be worthless, and the trader will lose their entire premium, which is the money spent to buy the option in the first place.

The premium is determined by taking the price of a call and multiplying it by the number of contracts purchased. This number is then multiplied by 100. Options trading can be complicated and risky for a new investor.

Bull Market vs. Bear Market

As you invest in stocks, you will hear the terms bull market and bear market very frequently. They describe what direction the market is currently going based on if things are going well or not. Suppose you ran into a bull or a bear while out on a stroll; you would take the situation very seriously. The same goes for if you hear either of these animals being described while investing in the stock market.

The bull market occurs when stock prices are going up and generally, means that investors are confident. This is a good sign for the economy as a whole. When a bull gores something, it pushes the horns up, just like stock prices going up. When the demand for a security far outweighs supply, which pushes the prices of stocks way up. In most bull markets, roughly 80% or more of stock prices rise over an extended period of time.

During a bear market, stock prices experience a prolonged decline. In a typical bear market, stock prices drop at least 20% amid widespread pessimism among investors. During this time, investors are fearful that the market will start to drop over time, so they begin selling their securities to avoid losing too much money. When a bear attacks something, it comes down with its paws, just like the stock prices going down.

There are various indicators that investors use to determine a bull vs. bear market, including wage growth, hiring practices, interest rates, and inflation. When investors see an economy shrinking, such as companies laying people off, it can signal a major decline ahead. A bear market usually follows a bull market and vice versa. The good news is, a bull market typically lasts must longer, 1,742 days, on average, compared to 363 days for a bear market, on average.

Assets vs. Liabilities

You will hear the terms assets and liabilities a lot in the investment world. Basically, assets add value to a company and increase the overall equity. Examples of assets include:

- Cash
- Inventory
- Office Equipment

- Real estate
- Investments

Liabilities, on the other hand, decrease a company's value and equity. These can include:

- Any type of debt
- Taxes owed
- Wages owed
- Accounts payable

If a company's assets outweigh their liability, this reflects positively on their financial health. On the other hand, having more liabilities than assets can indicate poor financial health and even the potential for going out of business soon. Of course, you will usually have to assess businesses that have been around for at least a few years.

What Is a Corporate Action?

An action made by a corporation is any activity that brings some material change to the organization. This will ultimately impact its shareholders. Corporate actions can be events like a bankruptcy or liquidation, a firm changing its name, as well as dividends, stock splits, mergers, and acquisitions.

A mandatory corporate action is automatically applied to an investment, while voluntary actions require a response from the investor. Publicly-traded companies are often overseen by a board of directors who are elected to their positions. These individuals are usually the ones who approve any corporate action, which usually happens through a vote.

Mandatory corporate actions include things like:

- Stock splits
- Dividends
- Spinoffs
- Mergers

Voluntary corporate action can be something like a tender offer. In simple terms, this type of offer is a broad solicitation to purchase some or all of the shares held by the shareholders of a corporation. Any action like this requires the consent of the shareholders.

Dividends

You will hear the term dividends quite a bit when it comes to investing in the stock market. Dividends are simply payments that a company gives out to the owners of its stock. They are a way for companies to distribute revenue back to their investors and a great way for investors to earn income.

However, not all stocks will pay out dividends. As an investor, you will need to choose specific dividend stocks. Dividends are paid out per share. Therefore, if you own 20 shares of a particular stock and that stock pays two dollars in annual dividends, then you will earn 40$ per year. These dividends are usually paid out in cash to a shareholder's brokerage account. A few companies will pay dividends in the form of stocks.

It depends on the company, but dividends in the United States are usually given out on a quarterly basis. However, some companies may do it monthly or semi-annually. Dividends must be approved by a company's board of directors.

Stock Splits

A stock split occurs when a business divides its existing shares of stocks into multiple new shares. This method boosts a stock's liquidity. Even though the number of shares increases, the total value stays the same. The most common ratios for a stock split are 2:1 or 3:1. So, for each share an investor has for a particular stock, they will have now have two or three. For example, if they owned three shares of a particular stock that split 2:1, they would now have six shares.

The reason for a stock split is so a company can lower the trading price of its stock. This will make it more comfortable for many investors to purchase. Many investors, especially those new to the game, are more likely to purchase 100 shares of $10 stocks over ten shares of $100 stocks. The goal here is to increase investor interest.

Spinoff

You may have had a favorite television show in the past with many great characters. Suddenly, a character on the show goes off and gets their own series. For example, the show *Family Matters* was a spinoff of *Perfect Strangers,* and *Frasier* was a spinoff of *Cheers.*

A spinoff in the business world occurs when a company takes a portion of its operations and develops it as a separate entity. When a spinoff occurs, shares of the new company are distributed to the shareholders of the parent company tax-free. Therefore, investors in the parent company automatically become shareholders of its subsidiary.

One of the main reasons for a spinoff is that a company may have a profitable division that is not related to their core competencies. As a result, the organization can decide to put that division under separate ownership so the parent company and the subsidiary can focus on what they do best. Another reason for a spinoff is to increase the combined stock value of a parent company and its subsidiary, so it is greater than when it was one company as a whole. On many occasions, owners and management of an organization feel that the stock prices undercut the value of the separate divisions that a company holds. With a spinoff, their hope is that the stock value surpasses what it was when the company was one consolidated unit.

Spinoffs have been historically good for investors. On average, the parent company and its subsidiary outperform the market in the 24-month period following a spinoff. Those who are able to withstand the initial unpredictability usually leave with exceptional gains.

Mergers

A merger occurs when two companies combine on broadly equal terms to form a new legal entity. Mergers are generally done to expand a company's reach, develop into new segments, or gain new market shares. All of these are done in the hopes of increasing shareholder value.

The organizations that agree to merge are roughly equal in size and scale of operations. When a significantly larger company buys out a smaller company, it is known as an acquisition. The companies, in this case, are not equal. After a merger occurs, shares of the new company are distributed to existing shareholders of the original two organizations.

It is important to understand what corporate actions are because you will need to know how they can potentially affect the value of your stocks. Also, keep up with company news, so you are aware of any actions occurring down the line. As a shareholder, you will have the ability to influence some of them and at least benefit from the others.

What Stock Trading Teaches Us About Success

When you learn about stock trading, you also gain knowledge in other areas of life. The process is more than just about making money, even though that's the main objective. Investing in the stock market can teach you a lot about success and failure. You will learn a great deal about the world around you, and this can provide you with many benefits. The following are the many ways that trading in stocks will help you.

It Will Give You Knowledge of Multiple Niches

I expect that you will do your research before buying any type of individual stock. This research will give you inside knowledge of the company and industry it is related to. As you look into various sectors, like technology, medicine, finance, and economics, you will realize they are all interconnected in some way. More knowledge will make you a better trader and better prepared for other areas in life.

You Will Understand the Value of Hard Work and Dedication

There are reasons why some people seem to have the Midas touch, while others fail at everything they try. It does not just come down to luck. Picking the right stocks takes a lot of hard work and dedication, just like success in anything else does. You have to spend an immense amount of time studying, learning new strategies, and then taking the time to implement them. Finally, you must have the dedication to follow through until the end. Investing in the stock market does not come with immediate success. You will have many rises and falls along the way. This is true of any other aspect of life.

Imagine buying a gym membership and then never going to work out. By doing this, you do not see your investment through. The same holds true for the stock market. Don't just put your money in and then forget about it. See it through until the end. Unfortunately, way too many people follow this path.

Success Will Not Occur Without Challenges

There are many graphics out there showing what success really is. Many people view it as a straight line with an upward trajectory. The truth is, there will be many dips and valleys along the way because success never comes without its share of challenges. These challenges are not meant to stop you but symbolize how motivated you really are.

Many people believe they should quit when they fail. However, failure is a learning opportunity, just like success. As a trader, you will have several failures along the way, but these are stepping stones to success in the future. As you learn how to deal with challenges with the stock market, you will understand how to manage them in your everyday life, as well.

Prosperity Is Everywhere

As you learn how to buy and sell stocks and where you can go to do so, you will recognize how many opportunities there really are out there. The internet has opened the door for so many people to gain a better position in life. This was not the reality before, as so many opportunities were limited to a small segment of the population.

Your Location Does Not Limit You

Thanks to the internet, you can trade stocks from anywhere. From the comfort of your couch, you can quickly go onto your tablet and check stock prices. While hiking through the woods, you can jump on your phone and make a quick stock trade, as long as you have internet connectivity. Are you planning a trip overseas? Find a good Wi-Fi location, and you can continue to buy and sell your stocks.

The internet has revolutionized business as we know it, and this is not limited to investing in the stock market. Sadly, only a small percentage of individuals have taken advantage of these changes. However, you can jump on the bandwagon of online success.

Being Reserved Can be an Advantage

When you experience a stock market failure, you learn that being reserved is more advantageous than being aggressive and losing it all. You should never be ashamed that you are fearful of losing money. After all, it is your money we are talking about, and you work hard for it. While your growth will be slower, you will stay in the game longer, have less stress, learn from market inefficiencies, and obtain more success in the long run.

Never Stop Learning

If you pick stocks the right way, you will never stop learning. Gaining knowledge is the foundation of success, and any top expert in any field will tell you that once you stop learning, you stop growing. Warren Buffett, himself, is a voracious reader. No matter how much success he has gained, he never stops gaining more knowledge. You must follow this same philosophy. No matter how much you gain or lose, always challenge yourself by learning more.

Constantly investing in the stock market will teach you that becoming too comfortable will be a detriment to continued success. By always bettering yourself, you will be more prepared than most other people in any aspect of life.

Take a Multi-Faceted Approach

This philosophy is perfectly illustrated by investing in the stock market. Most losses that come from the stock market are the result of missing some key indicators of success or failure. Therefore, it is important to analyze a decision from every angle before pursuing it.

Most failures that occur in life, whether business or personal, occur because many important variables were missed. While you cannot be prepared for everything, you must be meticulous in your approach so that you can catch the unexpected as much as possible.

Money Does Not Buy Happiness

While it can be exciting to see massive gains with your stock purchases, this does not equate to genuine happiness. As you make more money in the stock market, it will become apparent that it is not the key to happiness. There are other aspects of life that are more important. That being said, using money in the correct manner can lead to a happier life for you.

For instance, if you use the money on things you enjoy, like traveling, having new experiences, giving to the needy, or living in your ideal location, it can affect your emotions in a positive way.

History of the Stock Market

There are many events throughout history that changed and shaped the stock market to create what we have today. The focus here will be on the stock market of the United States. While I won't go through everything, I will provide a chronological list of some of the major events that lead to the development of what we have now in terms of stock trading.

- On February 23, 1970, the U.S. investment market was born. The federal government refinanced all federal and state Revolutionary War debt by issuing $80 million in bonds. These bonds were the first publicly-traded securities in the country. This marked the birth of investment markets in the United States.
- On May 22, 1972, a group of 24 merchants met under a buttonwood tree on Wall Street to sign an agreement to trade securities on a commission basis.
- In 1844, the telegraph was invented, resulting in better communication with brokers and investors outside New York City. This helped broaden market participation.

- On April 9, 1861, the Civil War caused stock exchanges to suspend trading in states that were seceding.
- On October 20, 1863, the New York Stock and Exchange Board officially changed its name to the New York Stock Exchange.
- On August 27, 1867, the stock ticker was invented, which revolutionized the stock market by bringing current prices to investors everywhere.
- On September 24, 1869, Black Friday occurred because of the speculation of gold. This resulted in a market crash
- On April 22, 1903, the New York Stock Exchange moved to its new and current location.
- On July 31, 1 914, World War I caused securities exchanges around the world to suspend their operations to stop prices from plunging. The New York Stock Exchange ended up closing down for four and a half months.
- In 1929, the market crashed on an unprecedented level, resulting in the Great Depression.
- On February 6, 1943, women began working on the Stock Exchange trading floor for the first time.
- On October 19, 1987, Wall Street experienced one of the largest single-day crashes with a $500 billion loss. The Markets plummeted worldwide.

- On September 11, 2001, the worst terror attack on U.S. soil occurred. The market shut down for seven days.
- In September of 2008, the worst financial crash since the Great Depression occurred. This was largely due to the mishandling of subprime mortgages.

As you can see, the stock market has taken many hits since its inception and is still standing today. Historically, the stock market always comes roaring back. The first online trading platforms began emerging during the early 1990s. Now they are used by investors of all skill and experience levels.

Stock Market Pros and Cons

Just like anything else, investing in the stock market has its pros and cons. While I want you to focus more on the pros, I want you to be fully informed by also understanding the many cons that exist. By recognizes the disadvantages, you will be better prepared overall.

The Pros

Investing in the stock market comes with a plethora of benefits:

- You can take advantage of the growing economy. As the economy grows, so do corporate earnings. Economic growth creates more jobs, individual income, and sales. The more money that people are making, the more they will put back into the economy by spending.
- It is a great way to stay ahead of inflation as stocks historically have a 10% return on average. This is better than the average annual inflation rate. For this reason, you can continue to buy and hold even if the value temporarily drops. With the right investments, you will still have a positive return.
- It is quite easy to buy stocks, as you will see later on in this book. There are many different avenues you can take to purchase, sell, and trade.
- There are two ways of making money: First, you can buy at a low price and sell high. These companies are expected to have fast growth. Second, you can buy stocks from companies that pay dividends. These companies are expected to have more moderate growth.

The Cons

Of course, we cannot mention the benefits without also discussing the disadvantages. So, here they are:

- There is a certain level of risk, and if you are not careful, you can lose everything. Do not invest what you are not willing to lose. I will get into the topic of mitigating risk in the next chapter.

- If you are a common stockholder, which gives you the greatest potential for returns, you will also be paid last if a company goes broke or bankrupt.

- When you are buying stocks on your own, it will be a huge time commitment if you are doing it the right way. With all of the research and follow up that is involved, it is like having a full-time job.

- You will be on an emotional roller coaster, and it will be exceedingly difficult to keep your feelings at bay. It can be easy to sell out of fear or buy high and hold too long out of greed.

- You will have a lot of competition in the form of professional traders and institutional investors. Not only do these individuals have extensive knowledge, but they also possess sophisticated trading tools and programs, financial models, and advanced computer programs.

"Be fearful when others are greedy.
Be greedy when others are fearful."
-Warren Buffett

I hope you have a good understanding of how the stock market and investing works. Don't worry because I will get into more specific details about certain topics in the following chapters. Knowledge is power, and the more you have, the better off you will be. In the next chapter, I will be discussing the idea of mitigating risk as related to investing in the stock market.

The Stock Market

CHAPTER 2: INVESTING TO THE STOCK MARKET IS NOT PLAY A GAME OF CHANCE

Imagine wanting to learn how to ski. There is a tremendous amount of risk that comes from this activity. You can fall, break a bone, receive a head injury, or end up with something much worse. Before you set out on the slopes for the first time, if you do nothing to prepare and don't take the proper safety precautions, your chance of getting injured is much higher. If you receive a lot of training before going on the slopes for the first time, the chances of something bad happening decrease tremendously. The same concept holds true for many other things in our lives, including investing in the stock market.

No matter how prepared you are, investing in the stock market carries a certain level of risk. This cannot be eliminated completely. Life is unpredictable and even if you do everything right, things can still go wrong. This is a fact we all have to live with. The goal is to mitigate the risk to have a better chance of success on the stock market or in any other type of investment. The focus of this chapter will be, not how to play the gambling game that has surprised so many people, but a professional approach, which is the absolute priority of risk control, preserving capital and avoiding financial ruin, understanding which is the way right and wrong to tackle this activity and make it effectively a professional activity that has long-term prospects, even as a career

How the Market Rises and Falls

The stock market is a volatile entity, and changes can occur at the drop of a hat based on many factors. When you check stock prices in the morning, and again in the evening, the numbers can be vastly different. Many experts say they can time the market and know exactly when prices will go up or down. However, none of these experts have a foolproof method that is right all the time. That being said, there are several predictors that can be significant indicators of which direction the market will go. The better you understand these, the better you will recognize when stock prices will rise or fall. Once again, there is no guarantee, but the goal is to be as close as possible.

Basically, stock prices change due to supply and demand. There are a limited number of shares available for sale, and buyers must compete with one another for access to these shares. The more buyers that show interest, the greater the demand will be. The higher demand results in stock prices going up. On the other hand, when interest in a particular stock declines, there are fewer buyers who are trying to make bids. This results in less demand, and stock prices will drop.

Think about a few examples in everyday life. During Halloween, more people want to buy pumpkins. The demand goes up, and the price for pumpkins rises at the same time. During Valentines' or Mothers' Day, many more flowers are being sold, so you will be paying more for that bouquet of roses or whatever types of flowers you desire. Whenever the demand for anything product goes up, so does the price.

That being said, what determines stock interest? What events or circumstances lead to increased interest in a particular stock? The short answer is information. There is certain information out there that will pique an investor's interest, whether consciously or subconsciously. These pieces of information can include press releases, social media posts, news stories, media interviews, court cases, and general public opinion. Anything that can influence public opinion in one way or another will fall into this category. For example, a specific company may promote a new product they are creating, and this will create a lot of buzz around the world. This new product interest can also lead to investor interest. On the other hand, a scandal that becomes public can rock the foundation of a company to its core, which may result in public disgust. This can result in investors packing and leaving in droves.

Of course, investors will react to the data they receive in their own way, and what may sound good to one person could be completely devastating to someone else. Based on specific reactions, investors will either buy more shares, hold onto the ones they have, or even start selling them off. The reactions and resultant actions will be incorporated into the share prices, causing fluctuations one way or the other.

Furthermore, if the supply of a particular stock is very low, and the interest is exceedingly high, share prices can rise up quickly. An example of this occurred in 2018 with a company known as Tilray. Tilray was the first publicly-traded marijuana company on the Nasdaq Exchange. The share prices started at $17 when the company first went public, but the price soared up to about $300 per share in a short period of time.

To be a knowledgeable investor and become a good predictor of the direction stocks will take, you must remain up to date on market trends, follow the news on what developments are occurring with a company, and also read sales reports. Do whatever you can to understand the company you want to invest in and the best companies to stay with. This will take a lot of time and effort but remember that it's your money, and the goal is to gain the most profits that you can. Therefore, take in as much information as you can. It will serve you well in the long run in determining the value of a company and how share prices will fair.

Diversification

Imagine that you are investing $5,000 into the stock market. If you take all of the money and put it into the shares for one company, your entire portfolio is dependent on how that one business does. So, if the shares of that company double in price after you buy them, you just doubled your investment. If the share prices go down by 50%, you just lost have of your investment. Now, let's say you diversify a little bit. Instead of putting the whole $5,000 into one company, you spread it out between five companies and invest $1,000 in each. When share prices go up, you will benefit from the profits, but they won't be as great as when you invested in a single company. Furthermore, the potential for loss will also be reduced because your money is not reliant on a single organization.

This is known as diversification, which reduces your potential for growth, but helps mitigate risk. I always recommend diversifying your portfolio, especially when you are a new investor. Of course, you also don't want your money spread out too thin to the point you can't keep track of it all. Pick a handful of companies you can easily manage and keep track of. After doing your research, invest your money into the companies you believe in.

First of all, when it comes to diversification, determine what percentage of your total income and net worth you want to be invested in the stock market. Figure out what you feel comfortable investing in and set that aside. Once you determine this percentage, it's time to break it down further and determine what amount you want to be invested towards each company's stock.

Investing in the stock market is an inherently risky practice, as nothing is ever guaranteed. Going the diversification route will at least minimize the risk that is involved. Also, never become too comfortable with a company because you never know when things can take a turn for the worst.

The stock market has provided an average of 10% returns annually. While there were many ups and downs along the way across the spectrum of companies on the list, there was an overall gain in the long run. When you diversify, one of your companies may be performing poorly while the other two are rising. The rising stocks can negate the losses from the company with falling prices and still create a profit in your portfolio.

So, your options are to chase one or two hot assets that have the potential for exponential gains but can also lead to a tremendous loss or staying on the safer route by following average market returns. A single stock can certainly outperform the market overall, but it can underperform too.

Diversification provides a safeguard against economic, political, or social factors that can harm one company but benefit another. Always remember that one major event can change the trajectory of a company, and therefore, its economic future and share prices.

Common Mistakes For Newcomers

Common Mistakes

Even the most seasoned investors have their share of blunders. However, as time goes by, these mistakes become fewer and less severe. In addition, experienced investors are better at circumnavigating these mistakes and continuing to make profits. Basically, they are used to making mistakes and recognize what they need to do to correct them. At least, the successful investors do.

As a newcomer, making a mistake can be detrimental to your psyche. Having high hopes of making great profits can be dismantled immediately when errors result in significant financial loss.

I don't want you to be turned off to the stock market because of simple miscalculations that can be avoided. Therefore, I will go over some common mistakes that newcomers and even seasoned pros will make. Avoid these as much as possible, and you will be mitigating the risk of losing your investment.

Not Understanding the Investment

It can be extremely exciting to hear about a new hotshot company that will be taking over the world. Many different thoughts and feelings can cross one's mind as they begin investing in various companies, but these cannot lead to you not understanding the investment. By not understanding the company you are dealing with, you are missing a fundamental step for determining the company's potential by not gathering adequate information. Essentially, you are going in blind with the hopes of hitting a home run. While there is luck involved with investing, it should never be the sole thing you rely on for continued success.

Legendary investor Warren Buffett always cautions people about investing in businesses they don't understand. Never buy stock in a company until you understand their business model, which is the blueprint needed for their success. The bottom line is that unless you have studied a company well, do not bother putting your hard-earned money into it.

Falling in Love With a Company

Falling in love is important when picking your future spouse, dream home, or vacation spot. However, it is something that needs to be avoided when trying to invest in a company. This usually occurs when we invest in a company, and the stock prices go up. As a result, we fall in love and forget that reason for buying the stocks in the first place: for investment purposes.

No matter how much of a profit you gain, never forget the reason for buying the shares. If any of the fundamentals that first prompted you to buy into a company change, then consider what actions you must take, including selling the stock. Never fall in love with a company, no matter how well it does. Doing so will severely cloud your judgment, so it's important to remain objective throughout the investment process.

Lack of Patience

You have probably heard the phrase, "Patience is a virtue," throughout your life. Well, in terms of investing, it is definitely true. The goal of playing in the stock market is not so you can make some quick money overnight. That may occur in certain instances, but it should not become your main objective.

The issue for most people is that slow and steady will usually not produce immediate results, which is what most people are looking for. Instead, the goal is to have long-term gain. Slow and steady usually comes out on top, whether it's at the gym, in a career path, or investing in the stock market. The information I provide in this book is not a scheme to get rich quickly.

Always take a disciplined approach when it comes to the stock market. Keep your expectations realistic in regard to growth and the time it takes to achieve it. You may see certain stocks rise quickly in a short period of time, but that will be rare, even for that particular stock. True gains are obtained over time. Expecting anything else is a recipe for disaster.

Excessive Turnover

Jumping in and out of investments too often can result in excessive commission rates, which will eat up your profits. In addition, you will out on the opportunity of having long-term gains.

Trying to Time the Market

Basically, market timing is a trading strategy where participants will try to beat the market by predicting its movements. Based on their predictions, they will buy or sell accordingly. Attempting to time the market can also kill returns. It is extremely difficult to successfully time the market, and even experienced investors fail at it all the time. Don't even try going down this route when you are new to the stock market. Most of the returns on investment are due to asset allocation and not by the timing of the market.

Waiting to Get Even

Waiting to get even means you are holding onto a losing stock in the hopes it will return to its original purchase price. This mindset is a cognitive error that will make you a two-time loser. First, you will continue to lose money on an investment. Second, you will miss out on investing more in other potential winners by not pulling out your money quickly enough. You will hear terms like "buy and hold" or "hold on for dear life" from various investors. However, it is important to recognize a loser and get rid of it when you can.

Failing to Diversify

I spoke about diversification earlier but failing to do so is a mistake many new investors make. They are looking for that one big win that will take them over the top. Once again, the goal is a long-term gain and not getting rich overnight. A general rule of thumb is to not allocate more than five to 10 percent of investment capital into a single investment.

Emotions Involved in Investing

As humans, we are full of emotions. There is nothing wrong with having various emotions during certain situations, but we must learn to utilize them to our advantage. When it comes to investing in the stock market, we must learn to keep these emotions at bay and use objective reasoning while trading.

The stock market will fluctuate up and down constantly, and this can put you on an emotional roller coaster. In a single day, your emotions can range from excitement, happiness, fear, anger, panic, and worry. Anyone of these emotions can severely cloud your judgment and result in losing excessive capital while investing.

It is okay to acknowledge your emotions. It is quite natural to have them. The important thing is not to act on them. This goes for selling during a major drop in buying in the middle of a huge surge. These events might be temporary and can turn around in a heartbeat. This is why it's imperative to base decisions on objective research and information and not what you are feeling on the inside. Save your emotions for events in your life that warrant them.

Of course, all of this is easier said than done. The following are some techniques to calm your mind so you can make rational decisions.

Take Deep Breaths

This may sound a little strange, but taking deep breaths can actually slow down many of your physiological processes, like heart rate, blood pressure, and breathing, all of which intensify during heightened emotional periods. As you feel your emotions rise, stop what you are doing, and take several deep breaths. As you calm your nerves, you will also slow down your mind, and this will result in thinking with more clarity. Try to avoid making important decisions when you feel like you're on edge. Otherwise, you will make a lot of knee-jerk reactions rather than thinking logically.

Consult With an Expert

With any new venture that you go into, it is advisable to seek out a professional for some guidance. If you were to start a new workout routine, you could consult a personal trainer. If you want to start a business, you can talk to an experienced business owner or coach. The same holds true for investing in the stock market.

Consulting with an expert can help you recognize if you are making sound decisions. If you cannot afford a financial advisor, at least talk to someone who has experience with investing in the stock market and glean whatever knowledge you can from them. Just make sure that person is not a highly emotional trader, as well.

Remember the Past

When the stock market goes down, it is important to remember that it's not the first time it happened. The market goes in cycles, and historically, there are gains in the long run. The stock market has overcome many obstacles, like great recessions, depression, and catastrophic events like 9/11. It is a resilient entity, so even if it's going through a hard time, history tells us that it won't last.

Each time a major decline happened, the stock market eventually came roaring back with higher returns. Yes, seeing a steep decline can be gut-wrenching when you are experiencing it for the first time, but it's important to remain objective and view things rationally.

Think About Your Age

Age does matter when engaging in the stock market. A market drop actually benefits younger voters because it gives them the opportunity to buy stocks at a low price and hold onto them for the long haul. Of course, you still want to make rational choices when picking stocks because not all of them will rise.

If you are closer to retirement age, then your decisions become trickier. You have to be much more thoughtful with the stocks that you pick because you want the ones that will give you higher returns in a shorter period of time. This way, you can pull out your profits when you actually retire. You also have less opportunity for riskier investments than people who are far from retirement age.

Best Practices for Picking the Right Stocks

When you have decided to start investing in stocks, there are certain strategies you need to follow for best practices. While there is no foolproof method to pick the right stock every time, you can still do your best to be right as often as possible. Intelligent stock-pickers have a few major things in common:

- They already know what they want their investment portfolios to achieve. They are determined to stick with these goals but also adjust as necessary for greater success. However, their main objective stays the same.
- They remain abreast of daily news, events, and trends that will have a direct impact on companies and the economy as a whole. For example, wars, new technology, or shifts in national politics can all play a role in affecting the economy. The pandemic of 2020 may be the most significant example in modern times of an event drastically impacting the economy.
- They use their knowledge and goals to make informed decisions when buying or selling stocks.

While everyone's ultimate purpose for investing is to make money, we all have different specific purposes behind our portfolio. For example, some people may just want a comfortable retirement, others want to create generational wealth, certain people want to supplement their current income, and some individuals want to become the next Warren Buffett. Determine what your goals are and make your stock picks based on these potential outcomes.

It is important to keep up with market news and opinions. Get used to reading the financial section of a newspaper or app. Follow financial experts on television and hear what they have to say, as well. While it can be overwhelming to keep up with all of the world's events, it is necessary if you want to gain success in picking individual stocks. Investor presentation reports and corporate press releases are also good resources for continued analysis of various companies and industries.

Once you have determined your investment goals, the next step is to find companies that interest you. There are a few simple approaches you can use:

- Research Exchange-Traded Funds, or ETFs, which track the performance of different industries. Look for the industry that you are interested in and determine what stocks those ETFs are investing in. The official page of an EFT will disclose all of their top picks.

- Use a screener to filter stocks based on certain criteria, like industry or sector. Screeners give their users the ability to sort companies based on several metrics, like dividend yield or market cap.

- Search blogs, stock analysis articles, financial news releases, and other resources for news and commentary on companies in the investment space you have targeted. Always analyze both sides of an argument and don't only look at the information you want to hear. Be objective in your research.

These methods offer an easy starting point to help you pick a company to invest in. As you gain more experience, you will pick up other methods too.

Once you have determined the industry you want to be in and become familiar with the major players, it is time to turn your attention to investor presentations. These will provide an overview of how an organization makes its money. They will also provide forward-looking information on the expected direction a company or industry will take. You can also browse through company websites and online presentations. This process involves more in-depth research of a specific company to see if it might outperform its competitors and how.

After all of these steps, look at your list of companies that you are still interested in. You may have started with dozens but only ended up with a few after going through the above process. That's okay because it's better to make a few good investments than a large number of poor investments. This can be extremely time-intensive but save you a lot of money in the long run.

Individual Stocks vs. Fund Accounts

When playing in the stock market, you have the option of buying individual stocks through various exchanges or opening an investment fund account. When buying individual stocks, you have to research specific companies and then buy, however many shares of their stock that you want. For example, if a corporation's stock is currently at $100 per share, and you want to buy five shares, you will be spending $500. If the stock value rises to $125, you will have gained $25 per share, with a total profit of $125.

Buying individual stocks will always give you higher potentials for return, accompanied by greater risk. I will get into different ways of buying individual stocks later in this book. Another option for getting involved in the stock market is to open an investment or retirement account, like a mutual fund, index fund, or a Roth IRA. These types of accounts are generally created through a bank or investment firm. They provide a highly diverse portfolio account consisting of stocks, bonds, and various other securities. You have the ability to allocate your funds within these accounts based on how risky you want to be. For example, a higher risk account can consist of more stocks and fewer bonds.

These types of accounts are generally managed by a financial adviser. Overall, they are a much safer option than buying individual stocks, but the potential for large gains is much smaller. I will go into more detail about these types of funds.

Mutual Funds

A mutual fund is made up of a pool of money collected into an account from many different investors. The money is then allocated to various securities based on the owner's preferences. Stocks, bonds, cash securities, money market instruments, and various other assets will make up these accounts. The purpose of a mutual fund is to give individual or small-time investors access to a diversified and professionally managed portfolio.

When you create a mutual fund, you are buying the performance of its portfolio. Unlike buying individual stocks, having shares in a mutual fund does not give the owner any voting rights. Just know that a share of a mutual fund represents investments in multiple securities. For a fund with slightly higher risk but greater returns, place a larger percentage of your money into stocks and less in bonds.

IRAs

An IRA is an independent retirement account. In a nutshell, an IRA lets you save for retirement and get tax breaks along the way by getting various deferments. Just like a mutual fund, these types of accounts are opened through a bank or other financial institution. The three main types of IRAs include:

- Traditional: Where investments grow tax-deferred, and contributions are tax-deductible. You will have to pay taxes when you pull your money out.
- Roth: In this type of account, your money grows tax-free. The withdrawals during retirement age are also tax-free.
- Rollover: An IRA created by transferring money from another retirement account, like a 401(k).

Once you open an IRA, you can use the funds to invest in various stocks, bonds, and other securities. The growth over time depends on how you invest. Greater investment in stocks will usually yield greater returns. One of the disadvantages of an IRA is contribution limits.

As of 2020, you can add up to $6,000 per year if you are under 50 years of age and $7,000 if you are 50 or older. There are also penalties for withdrawing money before the age of 59-1/2.

The great thing about the accounts mentioned above is that you can own multiple securities at the same time without having to personally manage all of them. You can own numerous stocks in various companies, which can offset the volatility that each of them provides. In addition, bonds and other securities can help mitigate much of the risk. So, if certain equities in your investment account are performing poorly, they can be offset by other securities that are performing well.

If you do not feel comfortable buying individual stocks, even after completing this book, then various investment and retirement accounts like the ones above are an option for you. Of course, the remainder of this book will focus more on individual stocks.

Index Funds

An index fund is a passively managed investment account, which means a portfolio manager is not actively picking and trading stocks like they would with a regular mutual fund. The process here is that a fund manager will initially build a portfolio of various securities with holdings that mimic the profile of an index or the stock market as a whole.

The expectation is that the fund will match the overall performance of the stock market.

The most popular index in the U.S. is the S&P 500, but there are several others, as well. There are many advantages to a passive-managed fund, including lower fees. Since the index fund managers are replicating the performance of a benchmark index, they do not need to rely on analysts and other experts to assist in the selection process. Trades also occur much less often, resulting in fewer fees and commissions.

On the other hand, actively managed funds have larger staffs on hand and conduct many more transactions, resulting in greater fees. This drives the cost of business, which leads to higher costs for the investor.

Index funds also provide strong returns in the long-term. Since the stock market generally does well over time, so will most index funds. Passive funds are ideal for investors who like to buy-and-hold.

The problem with index funds is that they are vulnerable to market swings and crashes. The recovery time can take a while after a major event. There is also a lack of flexibility, low human element, and limited gains. If you open an index fund, expect to hold onto it for decades or until you retire.

The Benefits of a Financial Advisor

When you are trying to build your wealth through investments, spending money on a financial advisor can seem counterproductive. However, you should see it as an investment, especially in time and information. With investing, you have to spend money to make money. There is a lot to learn when it comes to finances, and a good advisor can be worth their weight in gold. Here are some of the to hiring a financial advisor to look out for your future.

Objectivity

I spoke earlier about the importance of being objective when picking investments. The lack of objectivity is one of the biggest mistakes that investors make, especially when they are new. It can literally wipe out your entire portfolio. Decisions driven by emotions can undo months, and even years of hard work and proper decision-making.

Professional traders pride themselves on maintaining an objective viewpoint and executing trades based on analysis that is free of emotions. With a financial advisor in your corner, you can be sure that objectivity is present with every decision. These professionals will also keep you informed, provide the necessary advice, and undertake investment decisions on your behalf without the risk of emotions getting involved. Objectivity is especially crucial when the market is a bit shaky.

Having a Full-Time Professional

Having a full-time professional in your corner can offer a wealth of benefits. For example, they will have a wealth of training, knowledge, experience, and qualifications that will be difficult or impossible to achieve on your own. You also have a life and career to look after, so taking on the responsibility of being your own financial expert can become burdensome. You should certainly remain informed to make sure you are not being bamboozled, but much of the weight will be carried by your financial advisor.

When trying to find a good financial advisor, look at their qualifications as far as education and certifications. Also, look at how much experience they have in terms of years in the field and the various clients they have helped. Finally, look at the reviews that people have left. If you have friends who have used good financial advisors, seek out their recommendations, as well.

Taxation

Tax laws seem to be getting more complicated by the day. This holds true for taxes related to investments too. Over taxation can end up eroding the gains generated by an investment. Suddenly, an investment that brought you great returns ends up harming your overall income.

A financial expert can help steer you away from possible tax implications related to investments by choosing the rights picks. They can also advise you on the latest legislation that will impact your taxes related to specific investments. Overall, the money you end up keeping can make up for the money invested in a good financial advisor.

Research

Unless you are somebody who genuinely enjoys doing financial research all day, it can be quite overwhelming and mind-numbing to do so. I am sure there are other things you would rather be doing. A financial advisor will spend the majority of their time doing research for you because it is their job. It is how they make a living. Therefore, they will look into the best opportunities for you based on your personal investment needs.

A good financial advisor will either have the right answers or know where to look for them. They will maximize their knowledge of industry, markets, law, and taxation, so you don't have to. Furthermore, they will often be assisted by other advisors, analysts, and experts to help bolster their research.

Relaxation

One of the greatest benefits of a financial advisor is having peace-of-mind. You can stay relaxed with the knowledge that an investment professional is taking care of the wide range of challenges related to investing that you would have to deal with yourself. You will have more time to yourself because you won't have to keep constant tabs on what's going on in the market. Investing in stocks can become its own full-time job, so hiring someone to do it for you will free up much of your time and give you more sanity.

While hiring a financial advisor is no guarantee, many common mistakes can be avoided, and major risk-factors can be mitigated. Always do your research when picking an advisor because it is ultimately your money that is being invested. When choosing a financial advisor, consider the following:

- Education and experience
- Certifications
- Fees (Hourly, monthly, annually, etc.)
- Conflicts of interest
- Standard of care
- Comfortability
- Public opinion and customer reviews

If you are entering the game of investing in any capacity, you are playing a game of chance to a certain degree. No matter how much care you take, the risk factor will always be present. The objective is to mitigate any type of risk as much as possible to increase your chance of success. My advice is to do your research, prepare ahead of time, and enjoy the ride that's ahead. Always remember that investing is a lifelong game, so look towards future success and not just short-term gains.

CHAPTER 3: THE BEST METHODS

I am sure that most of you have a favorite store you like to go to, whether it's to buy groceries, clothes, sports equipment, furniture, or jewelry. We all have our favorites, and this includes the various platforms for making stock purchases and trades. I spoke earlier about how the internet has made it much easier to invest in the stock market. There are numerous online brokerage firms that can be accessed instantly. Also, many of the top physical firms have their own websites and apps that make it easy and convenient to trade over the web.

Now that we have gone over the fundamentals of the stock market and how to mitigate risk as much as possible, I will get into various methods to start buying stocks as a newcomer. There are many firms and institutions you can use, and I want to make sure you choose the best one for yourself.

Top Online Platforms

There are a number of online brokers available, and new ones will continue to pop up. This can make it difficult to choose the best one for yourself. To make your decision a little easier, here are some individual brokers that are considered the best in the industry.

Fidelity

Fidelity is a top-rated platform for investing because of the well-rounded package of tools and order executions that are available. Fidelity continues to provide top-quality research and education to all of its clients while committing itself to lower their fees and other costs. The following is a breakdown of the many benefits that Fidelity offers:

- The company provides great trade executions for their investors. Over 96% of orders, on average, are executed at a price better than the national bid.
- There is a wealth of information available for the clients and extensive and customizable asset screeners.
- The cash that is uninvested automatically gets swept into a money market account, which contributes to a higher portfolio return.

The following are some of the cons related to Fidelity:

- The accounts are only open to U.S citizens or residents. Others cannot open an account with Fidelity.
- Traders and investors must manually refresh the data when using the website.
- The company has several offerings of securities but currently does not offer options or commodities.

TD Ameritrade

TD Ameritrade is one of the largest online brokers. It has become known as a friendly trading site for beginners and boasts a great mobile app. There are great resources that newcomers can access to get a great education on stock trading. There are numerous learning pathways to help clients understand everything, from basic investing to advanced strategies. With the company, you can open an account to just browse around without actually making a deposit. You can take advantage of this by accessing and browsing through all of the training tools.

The following is a breakdown of the many advantages TD has to offer:

- The educational offerings will help novice investors become more comfortable.
- In addition to online education, there is also in-person education located at one of the 280 offices.
- They have an optimized website and mobile app to help clients quickly access their account details.
- Streaming real-time data on the mobile app is unlimited.

The following are some of the cons associated with TD:

- Some investors might have to use several platforms to utilize preferred tools.
- It offers one of the widest selections of account types, and this can be confusing to new investors.
- Funds are not automatically moved into a money market account, so investors will earn a small interest rate unless they take action to move their cash assets into a higher-yielding account.

Vanguard

Vanguard is considered the king of low-cost investing, so buy-and-hold investors can benefit greatly. However, the broker lacks a strong trading platform, which makes it difficult for active traders. The company has a solid reputation for below-average expense ratios. Vanguard is most suitable for the following:

- Long-term investors and retirement accounts.
- Individuals who prefer low-cost investment methods and don't mind limitations on active trading.
- Exchange-traded funds and index funds.

Even though it cost zero dollars to trade stocks, the brokerage site has been focused on buy-and-hold investors for so long that they never built up a strong, active trading platform.

If you are looking to go the active route, you may want to try a different platform. If you are interested in creating retirement accounts, then Vanguard is the place for you.

E*Trade

E*Trade will appeal to many traders because of the variety of services they offer. The broker offers many advantages and some disadvantages, too, compared to other platforms. The following are some of the pros to E*Trade:

- They offer great customer service as representatives are available 24 hours a day, seven days a week.
- The website offers an online chat feature, giving you easy access to an associate without having to make a call.
- There are numerous branch locations throughout 17 states for those who want in-person attention.
- They offer great portfolio management services.
- There are discounts available for active traders who trade multiple times in a month.
- There are numerous learning materials on the website, as well as in-person events at branch locations.
- They have an exceptionally large selection of mutual funds, well over 9,000 different types.
- Their EFTs are available with zero commissions.

- They offer great trading and option tools, like an options analyzer.

The following are some of the cons of this broker site:

- It is a little more expensive than other cheaper brokers. For example, options are 65 cents, and mutual funds are $19.95. Firstrade and Webull don't have any commissions.
- There is a $500 minimum requirement to open an investment account. TD Ameritrade and Webull have no deposit requirements.
- There is a limited number of stock reports, which also limits options for analysis.
- They have an annual fee for portfolio management.

Robinhood

Robinhood is a free-trading app that offers stock trades, EFTs, options, and cryptocurrency. There are no commissions or fees involved, which is extremely attractive to investors. Robinhood was once known highly for offering free trades; however, since 2019, many other brokers have jumped on the bandwagon, which has reduced the attractiveness of Robinhood. The platform is still solid, though.

The following are some of the pros to Robinhood:

- There is no account minimum.
- They have a streamlined interface, so you can quickly execute trades.
- One of a few brokers that offer cryptocurrency trading.
- Great for mobile users because of their easy-to-use app.

Here are some ways that Robinhood falls short:

- They have limited securities and don't offer bonds or mutual funds.
- There is no automatic dividend reinvestment program.
- For investing, they only support individual taxable accounts.
- There is no customer support over the phone, as all interactions must be done through email.

Webull

Webull is a brokerage firm that offers stock trades for zero commission. They are currently Robinhood's biggest rivals in regard to free service. They are ahead of Robinhood when it comes to research and analytics, as they originally started out as a research firm before getting into the brokerage industry.

The following are some of the major advantages of Webull:

- Free EFTs, options, and stocks. There are no inactivity fees.
- Opening an account is easy, convenient, and fully digital.
- The trading platforms are well-structured and simple to use.

Some of the disadvantages of Webull include:

- Their product portfolio is limited as they only cover US stocks, EFTs, and options.
- There are no live chat services, and telephone support is poor.
- There are no credit/debit cards or electronic wallets available for money transfers.
- Only bank transfers can be used for deposits or withdrawals.

Firstrade

Firstrade is a great discount broker that offers free stock and options trading. They also charge zero commissions on mutual funds, which no other broker can match. Finally, there is no contract fee for options traders. This is also unique to the industry. The only real setback with Firstrade is that there's no 24/7 customer support.

Charles Schwab

Charles Schwab is a well-known name in the investment world. It has many educational resources and tools for both new and experienced traders. The firm delivers for every type of trader and $0 commissions.

The following is a summary of the benefits Schwab provides:

- There are two platforms with no minimum deposit to open an account and zero fees.
- They have a user-friendly mobile app that is highly regarded.
- There is a large selection of funds.
- There are many physical locations available.

Merrill Edge

Merrill Edge is associated with Bank of America, so clients can benefit from the integration of a well-known bank and investment firm. Merrill Edge is known for its great research, which is done by a third-party. There is also zero fees on trades and no account minimum when you open. With Merrill Edge, you get the benefit of trading online but also having onsite locations across the country. The only disadvantage is that investors will find fewer options for securities compared to other brokers.

TradeStation

TradeStation has a high-powered trading platform and offers $0 trade commissions. Their selection of trade securities is also quite large. Like Robinhood, they also offer cryptocurrencies.

The following are some of the pros for this platform:

- Comprehensive research is available on trading
- Commission-free stocks, options, and ETF trading
- They have a very active trading community
- Advanced tools are available.

The main disadvantage is that their mutual funds have a transaction fee.

Interactive Brokers

Interactive Brokers is a strong platform that attracts man investors with low pricing per share, low margin rates, and a large selection of securities. This also includes over 4,300 mutual funds that have no transaction fees. There is a zero minimum deposit if you want to open an account.

The main disadvantage is that their website can be hard to use.

I am not recommending one trading site over another. I simply wanted to provide you information on all of these brokerage options so you can make a sound decision for yourself based on your needs. As you can see, there is no perfect choice, but go for the one that fits you best. You don't have to limit yourself to the above brokerage firms. There are several more available, but these are some of the most well-known and advantageous ones.

The Process of Investing in Individual Stocks

I already discussed earlier about developing your investment goal. This will determine how you will proceed with your trading strategies. Do you plan to make investing in the stock market your life, do it as a side income, or create long-term wealth and generational wealth? Whatever plan you decide to take will determine some of your strategies, including how aggressive you want to be. A few steps you should take before you dip your feet into the stock market include:

- Making sure you are secure with your employment. You should have a stable income coming in to take care of your other financial obligations while you begin investing.
- If you have a substantial amount of debt, I recommend you pay it down or even pay it off completely before proceeding with the stock market.

- Determine if your family situation will allow you to be a little risky with your finances and whether or not you will have time to dedicate to learning about stocks.
- What is your household budget? You should have a certain amount of your budget directed towards investment ventures.

Put Some Money Aside

Before you begin risking money in the stock market, make sure you have some cash reserves set aside in case of emergencies. I recommend having at least three months, but preferably, you should have at least six months' worth of emergency cash saved up and put aside. Also, put this money into some higher-yielding accounts like certificates of deposit or money market accounts.

The purpose of cash reserves are:

- Having an emergency fund in case your income gets disrupted, and you do not have to pull money from your retirement budget.
- Keep you from packing it in case your investment takes a nosedive.

Before you start investing, build up a healthy savings that you are comfortable with. You should be able to live comfortably off of your savings.

Get Some Financial Education

While you are saving up your money and building up your safety nets, you can get a head start by getting some financial education. This way, you have a general idea of what you are getting into. Many brokerage firms out there offer top-quality education. Also, local community colleges offer classes on investing, and you can visit many investment websites of financial experts.

Vanguard is a great resource and potential platform to use when you are ready. To become a good investor, you need to immerse yourself in that world. The old adage of becoming like the people you hang out with definitely applies here. Therefore, surround yourself with successful investors and experts and learn all that you can. As you will see, investing has its own language, and the idea is to become fluent in it.

There are many online courses you can take through sites like Udemy, as well.

Invest in Individual Stocks Gradually

Before you begin investing in individual stocks, you can gain more experience by opening safer retirement accounts, like an IRA or index fund, to learn more about how the process works. Once you are ready, you can open an account with one of the brokerage sites I mentioned above or anyone that you have researched and feel comfortable with. Determine if you have enough capital needed for the minimum deposit if there is one. As you go through this book, you will learn more strategies on how to pick the right stocks, including the methods the top-level stock investors use.

Here is a quick summary of how to purchase that first stock:

- Open your brokerage account with your desired broker.
- Decide what stocks you want to buy and how many shares of each. If a particular stock share is worth $50 and you want to buy four shares, that is a $200 investment in that stock alone.
- Decide what stock order type you want:
  - Market Orders: You will buy the stock at the current market price.
  - Limit Orders: You can negotiate a lower price per share of the stock based on your limit. For example, if a stock is selling at $90 per share, but you think it's worth $85 per share, you can

set that as your limit and see if the broker will sell it to you at that price.

- Optimize your portfolio by continuing to invest in various stocks. My hope is that stock market investing becomes a lifelong journey for you.

Don't Forget to Diversify

Are you thinking about putting all of your investment capital on that one promising stock, expecting it to become a winner? Well, think again. Unless you get lucky, you are picking a losing strategy here. Also, it is very risky to put all of your money into one investment, so it's much better to diversify.

Prior to investing in individual stocks, if you were already stocking up your various investment accounts, like your IRA, index fund, or mutual fund, then you are familiar with how diversification works. You do not have to get rid of these when you start investing in the stock market. In fact, it is better if you keep them and just further build your portfolio.

From here, you can pick various stocks from the online broker that you choose. For example, spread out your capital in five different companies based on your assessment of each one. This method will allow stocks that are performing well to offset those that are not. In a perfect scenario, all of your stocks will be doing well, but that's not always the case.

Monitor Your Stocks

From here, you will monitor your stocks on a regular basis. Of course, rather than daily activity, you want to focus more on monthly, quarterly, and annual results. As you will see later on in this book, it will be more beneficial to monitor the individual companies from where the stocks come from, rather than what they are doing in the actual market. An organization's performance levels will be a greater indicator of long-term success.

Why Should You Start Investing Now?

The earlier you start, the better off you will be with investing in the stock market. The longer you can keep your money invested, the more time it has to grow. Furthermore, if you start earlier, you can be a little riskier because there will be more time to recover. Many financial experts will tell younger people to focus on slightly riskier investments than someone who is closer to retirement age.

You probably wish that you would have started sooner. Don't worry about that now. Of course, the best time to begin was years ago. The next best time is now, so get started as soon as you can. Hopefully, that will be right after completing this book.

Where to Get Capital

No matter how you begin in the stock market, you will need a certain amount of capital to get going. The amount you need will depend on the particular requirements of the broker, as well as the costs of the stocks you want to purchase. For example, some brokers may require a $1,000 minimum to get started, while others will require zero, and you will just need enough to buy a single share of a particular stock. The following are some simple ways to obtain capital for you to start investing in the stock market:

- The most obvious method is to work and save money until you have capital.
- You can borrow money from a banking or financial institution. Some credit cards also offer interest-free financing for a certain amount of time. Be aware of any fees that could eat up your profits if you do this route.
- Start a crowd-funding campaign. You could advertise it as a new business, which stock market investing truly is.
- Borrow money from a friend or family member. Once again, be careful if you are going this route. Borrowing money from people you are close to is not always easy and can change the dynamics of a relationship. Make a solid plan for how you will pay the money back. Will they expect interest?

- Sell items you no longer need or want to raise extra capital. You may be able to find a gold mine by decluttering your living space.

Are you enjoying this book so far? If so, I'd be really happy if you could leave a short review on Amazon; it would mean a lot to me! I'm glad you have made it to this point. Don't worry, we are just getting started. Thank you!

What's Your strategy?

CHAPTER 4: TRADE LIKE THE BEST

How many millionaires do you know who have become
wealthy by investing in savings accounts? I rest my case."
-Robert G. Allen

Let's bring ourselves into reality here. People do not become millionaires by simply putting money away in the stock market. They either created enough interest in something or invested appropriately to make their wealth grow. The top investors in the stock market became millionaires and billionaires because they were willing to take heavy risks. They did not stow their money away in a savings or checking account. Those were old school methods. In order to build wealth like these individuals, you must be willing to do what they did, and that's to invest regularly.

Believe it or not, stock market millionaires are not just a bunch of elites living in high-rise buildings in Manhattan. It would be that grandfather living in rural Nebraska, the young professional who is just out of school, or the single mom who works part-time while playing the stocks. The advent of technology and the numerous online brokers, like the ones I mentioned in the previous chapter, has made it easier for everyone to get involved and profit from the stock market.

However, I do not want you to become overconfident. It has become simple to invest in the stock market, but it's still not easy. You will need the right strategies to perform well, even though much of it is not a game of chance. There are certain techniques that top-level investors have up their sleeves. The focus of this chapter will be to discuss some of the biggest earners in the stock market and lay out some of their strategies.

Warren Buffett

I have mentioned Warren Buffett throughout this book and for a good reason. He is arguably the greatest investor in the stock market of all time, as well as the owner and founder of Berkshire Hathaway, an investment firm based in Omaha, Nebraska. Of course, based on what he has accomplished over many decades, I don't see how it is even an argument that he is the best. He is consistently ranked near the top of the Forbes' list for the wealthiest people in the world. A few times throughout the years, he even became number one.

Even Mr. Buffett is not perfect, though. He has made many blunders throughout the years and still does to this day. His blunders generally cost millions of dollars, but he has that kind of money to lose. It just goes to show you that you are never immune to losing money while investing. However, the more you educate yourself, the more likely you are to have long-term success.

Warren Buffett follows a value investing approach. He looks at the company as a whole, so he chooses stocks based on the overall potential of an organization. This is done by analyzing a company's fundamentals. Value investors are similar to bargain hunters who shop at various locations looking for the best deals. An investor will search for stocks believed to be undervalued by the market. These are stocks that appear to have high value but are not recognized by the majority of the buyers. Have you ever had a friend who seemed to find great deals everywhere? Well, if you want to become like Warren Buffett, you must learn to do the same thing with stocks.

Mr. Buffett goes against the grain a little bit when it comes to value investing. Many of these investors believe that stocks always trade at their fair value and not the market value. This idea makes it more difficult to buy undervalued stocks or sell them at an inflated price. Mr. Buffett, however, is not fixated on the supply and demand measures of the market. Therefore, instead of seeking capital gains from soaring stock prices, he is more interested in whether a particular company is of high quality or not.

In summary, when Warren Buffett invests in a company, he is more concerned with how well that business performs, and it's potential to make money. He is not overly worried about whether the market will recognize its worth. How does Mr.

Buffett gain the information he needs? There are a few aspects of an organization that he analyzes before determining if they are worth the risk. Let's look at certain areas of his approach.

Company's Performance

Warren Buffett always looks at a company's ROE, or Return On Equity, which reveals the rate at which stockholders earn income on their shares of stock. Equity refers to the stocks an investor owns. This gives him a good indication of how well a company has performed consistently in relation to others in their field.

ROE is calculated by taking the net income and dividing it by the shareholder's equity. This needs to be a long-term assessment, going back at least five to ten years to get a good performance evaluation.

Company Debt

The debt-to-equity ratio is another major factor that Mr. Buffett considers when evaluating a business. A company that has a small amount of debt is always preferred to one with a large amount of debt. This indicates that earnings are being generated through the equity of shareholders and not from money that is borrowed that will need to be paid back.

This ratio is calculated by taking the total liabilities and dividing them by the shareholders' equity. The result will show the proportion of debt and equity the organization uses for financing its assets. The higher the ratio, the more debt is financing the company. Unfortunately, a debt level that is too high can make it difficult to pinpoint earnings because they will be very volatile and contain large amounts of interest. Therefore, look for businesses that have lower ratios, and you will be dealing with more equity.

Profit Margins

Looking at the profit margins of a company is crucial. However, we must not just look at a stationary number, but whether it is consistently increasing or not. This is calculated by taking the net income number and dividing it by the net sales. Investors should look back at profit margins for a minimum of five years. If the organization's margins are increasing steadily over the years, it is a good indication that they are efficient at controlling expenses. You definitely want to make sure a company is successful in this regard, and they show a positive pattern of it. Otherwise, you could be saying bye to your money real soon.

Is it a Public Company?

Warren Buffett usually does not look at companies with an initial public offering as he mostly considers investing in established companies. The minimum time a company needs to have been around is typically ten years. Any business younger than this would not typically be on his radar. Mr. Buffett shies away from many of the technology companies of today because he does not understand the mechanics behind them. If he does not understand a company well, he will not invest in it.

The philosophy behind value investing is identifying companies that have stood the test of time. These companies remain undervalued by the market, but investors like Mr. Buffett will still see the potential benefits. Therefore, if you are to follow the same methods, a company should have been public for a significant amount of time.

Always remember that a public company is obligated to file regular financial statements. It is a requirement of the Securities and Exchange Commission. Accessing these documents is a great way to analyze important data related to an organization. You can truly evaluate present and past performance that will help you make critical investment decisions. Obviously, the longer a company has been around, the more data you will have to work with.

Commodity Reliance

Warren Buffett tends to stay away from companies whose products are indistinguishable from their competitors. He is not so much interested in a particular commodity, like gas or oil, but in how unique a company's products or service is. Basically, do they stand out among the crowd? Mr. Buffett believes that the more positive attributes a company has that set it apart, the greater its economic advantage. This will make it tougher for any competitor to gain a market share.

Stock Expense

This is an important skill that Mr. Buffett possesses and may also be the most difficult to master. To begin with, an investor must determine a company's intrinsic value or worth. This is done by analyzing several business fundamentals, like earnings, revenues, and assets. A company's intrinsic value is generally greater than its liquidation value, which is its worth if it were broken up and sold today. This is because liquidation value does not take into account things like the value of the brand name or other intangibles not reported on a financial statement.

After Mr. Buffett determines the intrinsic value of a company, the next step is to compare it to the company's total worth, which is known as market capitalization. I will admit that Mr. Buffett has mastered this calculation over many years, and simply knowing the basics will not put you at his level. However, you can at least understand where he comes from and get a head start compared to other investors.

Warren Buffett's methods are not foolproof; however, they have resulted in him becoming a billionaire many times over. Basically, this approach reflects a practical method that is very down-to-earth.

Along with the above criteria, there are some simple rules that Warren Buffett follows, including:

- Determine what your reasons for buying a stock are based on personal criteria, like price.
- Invest in companies and industries you are familiar with. This will make it easier to stay current on trends and company news.
- Remain in cash holdings if there are no companies that pique your investment interests.
- Once you purchase stock in a company, follow that company on a monthly basis. Avoid looking at them daily because this will give you very little information.
- When a company no longer fits your criteria for buying their stock, it may be time to sell.

One major advantage that Warren Buffett has above everyone else is discipline. He has his set of rules and follows them diligently.

A great example of value investing was purchasing Apple stock in 2008. The market was down during this time, and the stock price fell from $172 to $97 per share. However, there were still a lot of people buying iPhones and other Apple products, eventually leading to stock prices soaring. The company has also had multiple stock splits over the years. 2008 would have been a great year to hold onto your Apple stock and even purchase more shares. This goes to show that you cannot always trust market trends, as many value investors do not.

Jack Bogle

Jack Bogle was a major player in the investment world, who passed away at the age of 89. While he is not as well known in the mainstream as Warren Buffett, he was still popular in his own circles. He was the founder of Vanguard, which is one of the most respected financial services companies out there. He is also known as the father of index funds, as he advocated for them for many years.

As a stock market investor, he was one of the best. For a good reason, too, because he had his own methods for creating his accomplishments. The following are a few philosophies that Mr. Bogle followed.

Be Comfortable With a 20% Loss

If you are having trouble imagining a 20% loss for you in the stock market, it is best not to get involved until you are comfortable with this outcome. That is because it could, and will likely, happen if you stay in the market long enough. The stock market is highly volatile and unpredictable, no matter how much pre-planning you do.

If you're going to invest in stocks, you need to understand that major drops will occur. The good news is the stock has always recovered over time. The recovery could take months or even years, but it will happen. This is why you need to invest for the long term and expect at least five years for any significant growth.

Play For the Long Term, Don't Beat the Market

Owning the stock market over the long term is what winners do but trying to beat the market is a loser's game. Much of this relates to actively managed mutual funds vs. index funds, which are more passively managed. Actively managed funds that have financial professionals carefully choosing what securities to buy rarely deliver massive results due to fees. In contrast, passive funds that mimic the stock market have much smaller fees over time.

Pay Attention to Companies, Instead of the Stock Market

This philosophy is similar to that of the value investor. Mr. Bogle believed that investors should focus less on the stock market and pay more attention to dividend returns and operating results of a company. As a stockholder, you have partial ownership in a company, and it's important to keep up with their progress. This is done b assessing certain factors, like their profit margin, market share, growth, competitive advantage, and future prospects.

The stock market goes up and down. If you are someone who checks it daily, you could see no real changes or major volatility. This could lead you to buy and sell constantly without considering the value of the company. As a result, you could lose out on a company by selling too quickly, or even hold on for too long and end up holding onto a loser. Understanding the fundamentals of a company you own share in and their potential for success in both the present and future, rather than just looking at market fluctuations, is what leads to greater profits in the future.

Don't Just Rely On Past Performance

While history can certainly give you a good indication of how well a stock will do, solely relying on this aspect is the wrong move for any investor to take. Any stock can have an amazing year, and it is no guarantee of future success. Many investors will get excited about a stock that soars over a short period of time and will jump in, expecting the same movement to occur. Remember, though, that one good year does not mean every year will be good. In fact, when stocks and other securities get ahead of themselves, they are likely to move back to reasonable levels and even lose market value. As a result, an investor who jumped in after a surge missed their opportunity for a major win. Also, if you are simply focused on past performance, you will miss out on major red flags that could indicate a stock plummeting in the near future.

The point here is that the past is no guarantee of what the future holds. Remain focused on long-term results based on company performance.

Pay Attention to Expenses and Emotions

When buying securities, whether in the stock market or through some type of fund, pay attention to the fees you are being charged at every level. Go the route that will provide you with the least amount of fees because these expenses can really eat into your profit margins.

On another note, it is also important to gauge the emotions of other investors. If you sense a widespread panic among the group, it is a good indication that they will sell their stock, and the prices will plummet. This will be a great opportunity to buy at a low price and benefit from major gains that occur.

Choose the Simplest Solution to a Problem

Many of us like to complicate things because we can never imagine that life is supposed to be simple. However, it is quite simple in many cases. Many people who begin investing believe they need to learn all of the ins and outs of the whole market and must become financial experts for the companies they are involved in. In reality, having a general idea of how a company is functioning, and their prospects for growth is usually enough. You can also just park your money in a reliable index fund for several years and have successful returns. You don't necessarily have to become a stock market expert to succeed in this area.

Buy the Whole Market Through Index Funds

Mr. Bogle was always a major proponent of index funds and believed it was a better idea to invest in a good index fund that basically buys the whole stock market. Opening an index fund will allow your money to follow the activity of the market, which historically does well over time. Therefore, rather than trying to find that individual winning stock, try investing the majority of your cash into an index fund and let passivity do the work for you.

Philip Fisher

Philip Fisher was a stock market investor who was synonymous with growth stocks. He wrote his bestselling book, *Common Stocks and Uncommon Profits*, in 1958. He had also started his own money management firm, Fisher & Company, in 1931. He was known as a prominent long-term investor who believed that people should invest in high-quality growth stocks.

There are many investment gems available in Mr. Fisher's book, but the most well-known piece of information is what he referred to as the "fifteen points to look for in a common stock." These points have become the holy grail for growth investors. Although Mr. Fisher did not expect most companies to meet all of the criteria on his list, he at least expected the majority of them to be covered. Here is the checklist of 15 points to consider before committing to your investment:

- Do the products and/or services that the company provides have sufficient market potential to make sizeable increases in sales that will last several years?
- Once the current products and services have been fully exploited, does the company have plans to continue developing various products or processes that will increase total sales potentials?

- How effective are the research and development efforts of the company based on their size?
- Is the sales organization of the company above average?
- How is the profit margin of the company? Is it worthwhile?
- Even if the profit margins are acceptable, is the company trying to maintain or improve the margins? If so, what actions are they taking?
- Are the labor and personnel relationships outstanding?
- Also, are the executive relationships outstanding?
- Does the company have depth to its management?
- How well does the company manage the cost analysis and accounting controls?
- What other aspects of the business, if any, give investors important clues to how outstanding the company may be in relation to its competition? Basically, how well does it stand out compared to others in their industry?
- Is the company's outlook short-range or long-range in regard to profits?
- Will the growth of the company require a sufficient amount of equity financing so that the larger number of outstanding shares will largely cancel the existing stockholders' benefits from the anticipated growth?

- Does the management of the company speak freely to its investors when things are going well but become silent when trouble is on the horizon?
- Does the management show unquestionable integrity at all times? Basically, are you never worried whether they are telling you the truth or not?

This 15 points strategy has helped generations of investors pick quality stocks for themselves. While no strategy is perfect, this one has certainly proven to be a winning formula. If you want to perform in-depth research on a company, following this method laid out by Mr. Fisher is a good strategy to take.

Benjamin Graham

Warren Buffett, who I spoke about earlier, is considered to be the greatest investor of all time. However, if you were to ask Mr. Buffett, he would say that Benjamin Graham is the greatest of all time. Mr. Graham was Buffett's mentor and is considered the father of value investing. He has written multiple books on investing and has come up with many principles that have helped investors throughout the years succeed in the stock market. I will go over some of his principles here.

Always Invest With a Margin of Safety

The margin of safety principle means buying a security at a discount compared to its intrinsic value. This method not only provides a high potential for return but minimizes the downside risk of an investment. This means that if the stock does go down further, you will not lose very much money. Basically, Mr. Graham's goal was to buy an asset that was worth one dollar for just 50 cents. He did this very well.

This type of value investing can lead to significant profits as the market will inevitably re-evaluate stocks and up their price to fair value. When these undervalued stocks were chosen carefully, Mr. Graham found that a decline occurred very infrequently.

Profit From Expected Volatility

The stock market being volatile is a given, and there's no way around it. So, you can either let it control you, or you can control the volatility. Instead of running for the hill when the market is under great stress, smart investors will use these opportunities to find great investments for a low price.

The stock market will offer different price quotes on a particular stock based on a number of factors. Instead of focusing on these prices, continue to look at the value of a business by examining the facts.

The market will fluctuate endlessly, but you can use this volatility to buy stocks at bargain prices and then sell them when they become too high or overvalued.

Know What Kind of Investor You Are

Examine yourself and determine what kind of investor you are. There are two choices in this area: active and passive investors.

Active investors can also be known as enterprising investors. This takes serious commitment in time and energy because there is a lot of research involved to ensure you make the right choices. You will have to engage in many of the activities I spoke about earlier, like reading financial reports, assessing the profit margins, and understand the various debt ratios. To be an active investor, you will need to do your homework on a regular basis. It is like having a full-time job.

If you are not up for this, then it may be better to take the passive route. You will have lower risk and will need to invest less of your time. However, you will also gain fewer profits. The bottom line is that the more work you put in, the greater the chances for a higher return. In the end, getting an average return with some type of passive fund, like an index, is much better than doing nothing.

Benjamin Graham spelled out in his book, *The Intelligent Investor*, some time-tested criteria for picking value stocks. Although this book was published over 70 years ago, the strategies still work to this day. The objective of his methods was to help find stocks that are poised for stellar price appreciation.

Quality Rating

Mr. Graham recommended finding companies with an S&P rating of a B or better. This shows that the company is average or better—the ratings of this system range from D to A+. To be as safe as possible, you can pick stocks with a minimum of a B+ rating.

Debt to Current Asset Ratio

The debt to current asset ratio should be less than 1.10. It is important to invest in companies with a low debt load because it will lead to better profit margins in the future. This ratio can be found through various services, like the S&P or Value Line.

Current Ratio

This is the current asset to liability ratio, which should be greater than 1.5. The more assets a company has compared to liabilities, the better. Many investment services will provide this information.

Positive Earnings

Find companies that have positive earnings per share growth during the past five years with no earnings deficits. The most recent earnings need to be higher than what they were five years ago. Companies with earnings deficits are high-risk and should be avoided as much as possible.

Price to Earnings Per Share Ratio

The price to earnings per share ratio should be at 9.0 or less. The lower this ratio, the more likely you are getting the share at a bargain price. This often eliminates companies with high growth.

Price to Book Value

The price to book value ratio is obtained by taking the current price of a stock and dividing it by the recent book value per share of a company. The book value is a pretty reliable indicator of a company's underlying value. It makes sense to purchase stocks that are selling below their book value.

Dividends

Find companies that are paying dividends and invest in them. If you buy an undervalued stock, it can take a while for the true value to be discovered, resulting in a long and tedious wait.

If the company is paying dividends, you can still collect some money while you are waiting for a stock to go from being undervalued to overvalued.

When considering purchasing a stock at a bargain price, also try to determine why it is selling at a bargain. For example, is it part of a dying industry? Was there an unforeseen problem, and is it short-term or long-term? Is management aware of any problems that exist, and are they doing anything to actively solve them? If you follow the above principle for value investing, you will be able to have success similar to Benjamin Graham.

John Templeton

John Templeton was another well-known value investor who was successful at buying while others were at their most pessimistic mindset. Basically, when most investors were turning away from the market, Mr. Templeton was getting great deals. For example, when World War II began in Europe in 1939, the legendary investor borrowed $10,000 to buy 100 shares each in 104 separate companies that were selling for one dollar or less per share. Many of these companies were in bankruptcy. However, a few years later, 100 of these companies turned around and led to huge profits. Four of them ended up being worthless.

Mr. Templeton understood the concept of value investing. He indicated in past writings that successful investors were not only intelligent when it came to picking stocks but also had their emotions under control. Emotional control allows them to go against the grain and not completely lose their minds. Additionally, they will be going against the grain for the right reasons and not just to be rebellious. The following are Mr. Templeton's rules for investing:

- Invest for a total return that is real. This means your return after things like taxes and inflation. Determine how much you will actually be making with an investment.
- Invest, rather than trade or speculate. Expect to hold onto stocks for the long run and not to just turn around and sell quickly. You could miss out on future profits and also incur many fees.
- Remain flexible and open-minded about potential investments. No single investment vehicle is a winner all the time. However, the S&P 500 has outperformed inflation, as well as treasury bills and bonds.
- Buy low, which means you may have to go against the crowd. It can be enticing to buy something when other people are getting excited about it, but this is where emotional control comes into play. In order to buy

stocks at a low price, you will probably have to wait until others are walking away.

- Always search for bargains among the quality stocks. A company should be well-positioned and well-rounded before purchasing its stock shares.

- Mr. Templeton emphasizes that individual stocks determine the market and not the other way around. Therefore, continue to buy based on value, regardless of what the market is doing.

- Diversify your portfolio with stocks, bonds, and other securities.

- Always do your homework when investing in the stock market. If you don't have time to do so, hire a trusted expert who can.

- Buy and hold is not the same as buy and forget. You should never buy a security and forget that it exists. Aggressively monitor your investments on a regular basis.

- Remember not to panic. Even if everyone around you is selling, it may be best to hold onto your portfolio, depending on what the situation is. Basically, do not blindly follow the crowd based on emotions.

- Always learn from your mistakes because mistakes can cost a lot of money. If you keep making the same ones over and over again, you are senselessly hemorrhaging money.

- Begin with a prayer. Of course, this advice is selective based on what people actually believe. If you believe in the power of prayer, then use it. If not, there are other methods to clear your mind, like meditation or deep breathing exercises.
- Always remember that outperforming the market is a difficult task. Even the greatest experts in the field have a hard time doing it.
- Never become overconfident and feel that you know everything. Trust me; you don't. When you start getting this mindset, you will begin to fall because unnecessary mistakes will start to occur.
- Never invest on a tip or a whim. You may get lucky once in a while, but do it too often, and you will lose more money than you gain. This is similar to playing the slot machines.
- Do not be overly fearful or negative. The stock market has been through a lot and always comes out on top. Optimists have always carried the way when it comes to stocks.

Peter Lynch

Peter Lynch is the former manager of Fidelity Magellan and is considered a legend in the mutual fund industry. Mr. Lynch has many pearls of wisdom out there, but here are some of the most valuable tips to create long-term wealth.

Invest In What You Know

This does not just mean buying stocks in companies you have done business with or enjoy the products of. Mr. Lynch is stating that you should do your research and understand the company before purchasing their stocks. Stay within your circle of confidence when investing in a business or industry.

Focus On the Companies, and Not the Stocks

It seems like we have heard this before. Never forget that you are a partial owner of a company that you own stocks in. If you owned a store or any other type of business, you would pay close attention to how it runs. Maintain this same mindset when owning stocks. Act like you are the owner of the company and pay attention to the fundamentals, like revenue, profits, and cash flows. These factors will ultimately determine the value of the company's stock.

Don't Be Distracted by the Stock Prices

What the stock prices do today, tomorrow, or next week serve only as a distraction. It is irrelevant what a stock does on a day-to-day basis. It is better to focus on quarterly or yearly financial results.

It Takes Years to Become a Big Winner

Except for a few outliers, nobody becomes rich overnight. Those that do usually don't stay rich for long. Life-changing wealth is made over many years and decades. Therefore, any time you buy a stock, expect to hold onto it for many years before you see maximum gains.

Do Not Become Fearful

Stocks should not scare you. Many people get rid of stocks because they become fearful of them based on news that they hear, which may or may not be accurate. Instead of listening to a bunch of pundits, rely on your own research to determine if a company's stock is worth holding onto. As a result, you can stand by your stock as long as the fundamental story does not change.

Time Is on Your Side

Investing in superior businesses can give you a valuable edge in the stock market. Companies that have strong advantages competitively will usually grow stronger over time while their competitors will slowly fade away. These businesses can generate tremendous profits over many decades, resulting in superior gains to your investment.

Don't Time Market Cycles

As always, timing the market is a loser's game. You can speculate all you want, but it is nearly impossible to know when a recession will be coming. Way more money has been lost by investors preparing for corrections than the actual corrections themselves. Instead, continue to hold onto your stocks as the market ebbs and flows, and just monitor the performance of the associated companies. When the market soars over time, the elite companies generally go with it.

Don't Expect to be Right, Even 90% of the Time

In the stock market business, if you are right six out of ten times, you are doing well. Don't expect to be right more often than this. You can certainly try, but don't get discouraged if it does not happen. The interesting thing about the stock market is that a few big winning stocks can offset and make up for losing stocks. For example, you can have a stock that loses %100 of its value but have another one gain over %1000.

What Should You Do With Your Money?

Peter Lynch was a major proponent of living life to the fullest. In fact, that is exactly what he did. After creating a lifetime of wealth, Mr. Lynch retired from the mutual fund industry and pursued other interests in life.

He stopped chasing money once he determined he earned enough. It is up to you whether you will do the same or not.

You may have noticed that I repeated myself several times. However, the greatest in the business often use similar strategies and learn from one another. A common trait that many top investors have is that they are less concerned with the activity of the stock market and more focused on what specific companies, which they have a certain interest in, are doing. Involve yourself with good companies based on adequate research, and you will see significant gains in the stock market. If you are perplexed about what to do with the stock market, follow the guidance of some of the best, which I have mentioned here.

CHAPTER 5: MAKING MONEY WITH THE STOCK MARKET

Make Constant Money!

When you think about it, it is a pretty simple process to make money in the stock market. You buy shares of a company's stock, hope that it goes up, and collect the profits whenever it does. Of course, that is a superficial description of what actually happens, and in order to be successful, there is much more at play.

The focus of this chapter will be to discuss various ways of making consistent income with the stock market.

By using these strategies, you can create some cash flow while you are patiently waiting for your stock shares to obtain massive gains. We have touched on a few of these strategies already but will get more in-depth in this section.

Passive income is one of the items we are talking about here, and this refers to a cash stream that requires little to zero daily effort to maintain. After an initial investment, you can start earning regular income without regular effort on your part.

Dividend Income

Dividends are probably the most obvious and simple way to make regular passive income with the stock market. As publicly traded companies earn their profits, a percentage of their profits get separated out and funneled back to their investors. These are called dividends. From here, investors can choose to take out the cash and pocket it or reinvest the dividends into additional stock shares. Reinvesting can create a type of compound investment machine if the stock continues to do well.

Dividend yields will fluctuate on a yearly basis and will vary significantly from one company to the next. The best dividend-paying stocks to choose from are the ones with a longstanding record of paying out substantial dividends.

There is a market index known as the S&P Dividend Aristocrats. This index includes select companies from the S&P 500, which:

- Have regularly increased their dividends over the past 25 years.
- Have a float-adjusted market cap of at least three billion dollars. This is where shares only available for purchase are weighted towards the market cap instead of total shares outstanding.
- Have an average daily trading value of at least five million dollars.

In summary, Dividend Aristocrats are large companies with high liquidity and stable dividend payments. Investors can pick out specific Dividend Aristocrats or pick out specific index funds that follow the S&P 500 Dividend Aristocrats.

Investing in dividend stock is like investing in any other type of stock. First, you will need to determine what stock you want to purchase. Many financial sites, including online broker's websites, will disclose which stocks pay out dividends. After screening several different stocks, compare their yields among each other. Be careful if a company's dividend yield is significantly higher than companies that are similar. It could be a major red flag that at least warrants further research.

Also, look at the company's payout ratio. If it is too high, like over 80%, it means the company is putting a large percentage of its income into paying dividends. A high payout ratio can result in the company going into debt. In addition to looking at dividends, choose your dividend stocks based on similar criteria as other stocks.

Once you have determined what you want to buy, decide how many shares of different stocks you want to purchase. Remember to diversify when buying individual stocks. If you can receive dividend payments from multiple companies, it will be great for your passive income. Pay attention to the dividend yield, as well. This should be the number one consideration because a dividend yield that is too high can indicate that the payout is unsustainable or that investors are selling the stock in high numbers, which will lead to a drop in price. Any yield over 4% should be looked at closely. Those over 10% fall into the high-risk category.

Once again, as your dividends are paid out, you can choose to pocket the cash or reinvest for more potential growth. In most cases, dividends are paid out quarterly. To give you an idea, here is a list of high-dividend stocks that are based in the US.

The number next to them is the dividend yield, based on the latest information.

- Altria Group Inc.: 8.7%
- National Health Investors Inc.: 7.45%
- Principal Financial Group Inc.: 5.43%
- Safety Insurance Group Inc.: 5.33%
- International Business Machines Corp.: 5.18%
- Bank of Hawaii Corp.: 5.0%
- Boston Properties Inc.: 4.92%
- Edison International: 4.53%
- M&T Bank Corp.: 4.5%

These are just some examples of companies that pay out the highest dividends for you to look into. If you play the dividend game well, you can continue to profit from passive income for as long as you want.

Momentum Stock Investing

Investing in momentum stocks entails buying securities that are on the rise with the intent to sell them once they have peaked. The idea is that these stocks are on a trajectory upwards and will continue to do so for a while. Basically, they have momentum, and your job as an investor is to ride that momentum for as long as you can. Your goal is to work with volatility and use it to your advantage.

Momentum stock investing goes slightly against the grain of buying low and selling high. This is because the stocks are already on the rise, and you just need to hope you catch it before the climax. Skilled traders know when to enter into a position, how long to hold, and when the right time to exit is. As a new investor, you may find this strategy a little intimidating at first. However, once you learn how to identify momentum stocks, you can earn quite a profit from them. This strategy can certainly create some passive income for you, but there will be a lot of active trading and monitoring involved.

There can be several risks to momentum trading, including:

- Moving into a position too early.
- Closing out too late.
- Getting distracted and missing out on major trends and deviations.

The proponents of momentum stocks, including Richard Driehaus, who is considered the father of this type of investing, felt that more money could be made through buying stocks high and selling higher than buying low and waiting for the market to re-evaluate them. Mr. Driehaus believed that the money from losing stocks would be better served on securities that were at a boiling point, right before they are set to take off. A true momentum investor looks to be the leader of the pack by being the first to jump on an upward-moving security.

The following are some of the major benefits of momentum investing:

- Potential for high profits over a short period of time. This philosophy goes against the main reason to invest in stocks, which is a long-term gain. However, lucrative profits can be made when momentum stock investing is done the right way.
- Leveraging market volatility to your advantage is a great way to get a high return on investment.
- Leveraging the emotions of emotional investors. Rather than being controlled by their own feelings, momentum investors learn to take advantage of the emotions of other people. If they notice people getting excited and buying certain stocks, they will jump on that trajectory and jump off when it's the right time to do so.

There are some common disadvantages to momentum investing too, including:

- High turnover, which can lead to expensive fees.

- It can be very time-intensive as you will have to monitor stocks on a daily, or even hourly basis, at times.
- It is market sensitive, and this strategy works best during a bull market.

Imagine momentum investing as jumping onto a train just as it starts moving, staying on while it is accelerating, and jumping off right before it comes to a screeching halt. Figuratively speaking, this is what you are doing.

While picking momentum stocks can be tricky, I will go over some methods to help make the process easier, and hopefully, more profitable for you.

Momentum Stock Scanning

There are many different criteria you can use to narrow down trending stocks that are actively experiencing momentum. You can use a stock scanner that will screen some securities and return a small list of potential momentum stocks. From here, you can analyze them further.

Earnings Growth

A common trend among momentum stocks is that they consistently report growing revenue. They also tend to outperform the predictions of most analysts when the earnings reports are released. To pinpoint stocks with accelerating earnings, look for those whose shares have increased consistently over every quarter for the last year. The most recent earnings-per-share was significantly higher than in the same quarter the previous year.

Higher Returns

A simple way to identify momentum stocks is to look at the ones that consistently outperform the market. Scan for stocks that are yielding higher returns over the past three, six, or 12 months than the common indexes, like the S&P 500. The first scan will yield many stocks. To narrow the list down, continuously remove the bottom 10% until your list is down to just a few stocks. Anywhere from five to ten is plenty. From here, you can investigate the securities further.

Positive Short-Term Averages

A momentum stock should be consistently trending upward. This means its short-term moving price averages are regularly higher than its long-term averages. Therefore, you can scan for those stocks whose averages are stacked according to their timespan. This may mean looking for stocks with a higher 10-day moving price average than a 50-day moving price average. Furthermore, the 50-day average will be greater than the 100-day average.

Always Setting New Highs

A momentum stock will frequently set new highs, only to continue breaking their own record. The objective here is to determine how your trading will compare to the timeline of highs. For example, momentum stocks that are regularly breaking their four-day highs should be more appealing targets than stocks breaking 30-day or 50-day highs.

Momentum trading will always be risky because it will never be clear how long an upward trajectory will last. It could last for months, or years, and then suddenly tank. In addition to the above strategies, pay attention to the news or major events. For example, the recent outbreak of the pandemic put a major hit on various businesses related to travel. If you notice the momentum slowing down, it is best to sell the stock rather than hold onto it overnight.

Insider Trading Secrets

I will briefly cover some insider trading secrets that professional traders use to help them gain more success in the stock market. The thing about insider trading is that it can be illegal in some respects, so you must make sure you do not cross this line. Otherwise, you could end up in a lot of trouble. My objective for this section is to go over some insider secrets that can help you but won't land you in hot water.

While insider trading is often frowned upon, it is not always illegal. In fact, it occurs quite often. To make it simple, if you receive information about a company that has not been made public and you use this information in your trading practices, then you are likely doing something illegal. Insiders are legally permitted to trade stock shares of any company that employs them, as long as the transactions are filed with the Securities and Exchange Commission, and advanced filings are completed.

If you work for a company, you will have an advantage as far as being aware of the insider secrets of what is going on. As long as you process in a legal manner, you should be alright. That being said, you can be an outsider and still benefit from the knowledge an insider has. How is this possible? Should you meet your friend for lunch while he shares all of the secret information about his company? Should you pay the CEO of an organization to give you information that is not publicly known so you can sell off your stocks before a big event occurs? I would not recommend this. Tactics like this will surely bring down some disciplinary action and even land you in jail.

There are some simple ways to get insider secrets, even if you don't work for a company. The great news is these methods are totally legal. Just go to a website like Yahoo! Finance and click on the "Insiders" tab to get a list of the latest trades going on within organizations. While some insider trading filings do not show up in various databases for at least a month, Yahoo! Finance seems to be very current on the most recent data.

Another option is to go to the Securities and Exchange Commission or SEC, Database, which is called EDGAR, where trading data is sent first. Once you are on the SEC website, search for the "central index key" or CIK for the company you want to search for. The CIK is used for the identification of corporations and individuals who have filed disclosures with the SEC. From here, you can search individual filing to learn the insider trading information you will need.

Insider trading is not a new phenomenon as investors throughout many years have been basing their trade decisions on the information derived. Be aware that a company could have hundreds of insiders, so trying to keep all of the information straight can become a struggle. Always perform your due diligence in assessing a company while paying attention to what insiders are doing.

There are several ways to make money in the stock market. In fact, many individuals become professional stockbrokers or simply find ways to earn income through the market. Of course, you can also choose to keep profits from the stock market as a side income.

CHAPTER 6: TRADING VALUE STOCKS

"...price is what you pay; value is what you get. Whether it is socks or stocks, I like buying quality merchandise when it is marked down."
-Warren Buffett

By now, I am sure you understand the value of "value stocks" because most of the major investors of the past and present swore by them. They were more interested in the quality of the company rather than the market as a whole. Consider this as an example. You go to a restaurant, and it's bustling. Everyone is raving about the food, service, and atmosphere. You get excited by what you see, but once you get your food, it tastes awful. At this point, do you care more about the positive attributes of the restaurant or that your food does not taste good? More than likely, you will be upset by the food, and you will not get that particular dish again.

Now, imagine ordering something else, and it tastes incredible. You will probably get that dish again, regardless of what is happening in the restaurant. You will continue to order this tasty meal and not the other one as long as it is still up to your standards. This same outlook should be used when purchasing stocks. It does not matter what the market is doing, but how well the company is operating.

Traditionally, value stocks are long-established companies with consistent profitability, revenue streams, and steady growth. They are companies that are not yet recognized for their value by other investors and the market as a whole. However, once they are, the stocks rise well.

The key to value investing is finding stocks that are undervalued, and very few people know about it. Imagine a guy giving away $100 bills for $70. This is definitely a great bargain, but it won't last long. Eventually, the seller will run out of these $100 bills as more people find out about them. The same holds true for value stocks. Make sure to read this chapter fully before investing in these securities.

Know the Terminology

Before you can succeed in a particular field, you must understand the terminology that is used. The same goes for value investing. In this section, I will go over some important concepts and terms to be aware of before investing in these types of stocks.

Intrinsic Value

This refers to the true value of a business based on a number of factors. This can be difficult because there is no one way to determine this value.

If you ask ten different experts, you will probably get ten different answers on how to determine intrinsic value. The calculations are quite complicated and are usually done by a financial analyst.

Margin of Safety

The margin of safety is something that limits the potential for losses. For example, a company that is trading for a major discount compared to the book value or one that pays above-average dividends. In either case, the investor is somewhat shielded from losing a major portion of their investment.

Economic Moat

This refers to a company having some sort of durable competitive advantage, which helps to protect its market share and lifelong profitability. Economic moats can come in the form of brand names, having variability of products, or cost advantages. For example, Coca-Cola has a strong brand name and a massive distribution network. There also multiple products around the world under the Coca-Cola umbrella. These advantages allow the company to move its products around the world more efficiently and charge a higher price.

Book Value

Book value refers to the value of a company's assets, minus the liabilities. These numbers can be found easily on a balance sheet. You can further determine the book value on a per-share basis by dividing this number by the number of outstanding shares.

The tangible book value excludes intangible assets, like intellectual property rights. It's difficult to tell how much things like intellectual property might sell for during the liquidation process. Therefore, the tangible book value can be used to incorporate a margin of safety when determining the value of a company's assets.

Cash Flow

A company's cash flow is the difference between the incoming and outgoing cash. If a company takes in $100 million dollars during a particular quarter and spends $60 million during that same quarter on investments, equipment, and other expenses, it had a positive cash flow of $40 million. All publicly-traded companies release a cash flow statement with their quarterly reports.

EBITDA

This acronym stands for Earnings Before Interest, Taxes, Depreciation, and Amortization. This information is used in several value investing metrics and is believed to give a more apples-to-apples version of earnings than simple net income. EBITDA can help account for various distortions.

Payout Ratio

The payout ratio helps investors evaluate the sustainability and stability of dividends that a company offers. This metric represents the percentage of a company's earnings that is paid out in dividends. For instance, a company earning one dollar per share that pays out 30 cents in dividends per share has a payout ratio of 30%. Obviously, the more a company earns, the more likely they can continue to pay out dividends.

The bottom line is that value stocks will not make you rich overnight, and that is not their goal. Instead, follow the motto of "slow and steady wins the race." Investing in the stock market should always be considered a lifelong pursuit and not an overnight success.

The Principles of Value Investing

Value investments have stood the test of time, and the strategies have created some of the wealthiest people in the stock market, including Warren Buffett. There are many different analytics and metrics you can use to determine the intrinsic value of a stock, but when it comes down to it, there are three main principles to value investing.

Do Proper Research

Don't even think about buying stock in a company until you understand it the best you can. Here are some criteria to follow when doing your analysis:

- Long-term plans
- Business philosophy and principles
- Financial structure
- The management team setup (CEO, CFO, etc.)

A big part of value investing is to focus on companies that pay out dividends regularly. This is because profitable companies often give back to their investors. Intelligent value investors also look past an organization's short-term earnings. These earnings will tell them nothing about the company's overall value. Unlike momentum traders, which I spoke about in the previous chapter, value investors are not interested in the media hype of a company.

Diversify

The common word today for investing is "diversify." Always find ways to diversify your securities, so you don't place all of your capital on a single entity. Don't put all of your eggs into one basket, and you will be protected from serious losses.

Look for Steady, Not Extraordinary

New investors want to make money fast. If this is your goal, you can try momentum stock investments, but you will be taking a huge risk by doing so. There are so many articles out there giving stock advice or listing specific equities every investor should own. You may have noticed that I did not do that in this book. My goal was to never tell you what to invest in, but how to pick your own investments.

Therefore, avoid going extraordinary and stick with steady. This will take time, effort, and patience, but you will have better returns over the long run. You may find a couple of stocks that will explode and make you a lot of money. This strategy will eventually fail, so count your blessings when it happens, but stick to steady investment strategies. An intelligent investor will be satisfied with low-risk securities that provide consistent returns.

Don't Follow the Herd

There are plenty of mistakes you can make in the stock market. Before buying a value stock, you should never follow the herd. Value investors are contrarians in their own way, so they reject the efficient-market hypothesis. In addition, when others are buying, they are usually selling or standing back. Value investors definitely do not buy trendy stocks because they are usually overpriced due to all of the interest.

If the financials back up a company, they will usually invest in companies that are not household names. When you get into value investing, never blindly follow the crowd, or you will be led astray. Instead of buying undervalued stocks at a bargain, you will be purchasing securities that are highly overpriced. When you get into this method of trade, follow the path of the most successful in the field, and you will find yourself only following a few people.

I hope you enjoyed this final chapter on value investing, one of the most effective trading strategies out there.

CONCLUSION

Thank you for making it through to the end of *Beginner's Guide to the Stock Market*, let's hope it was informative and able to provide you with all of the tools you need to achieve your goals, whatever they may be. The stock market has been around for decades and has gone through many different events. It has also changed in many ways throughout time, but the one thing that remains consistent is that it has always recovered, no matter what challenges it went through.

Back in the day, making decent money in the stock market was a faraway dream unless you were already connected to that world in some way. The stock market was an entity that the richest among us got to enjoy, while the majority of the population had no clue what was happening. With the advent of technology and increased access to information, getting involved in stock trades has never been easier. With the flip of a phone, you can log onto various apps or websites for different brokers and begin buying and selling various securities almost immediately. All you need is enough capital.

Of course, investing in the stock market is a simple process, but it is not easy. It comes with many challenges and those who do not take it seriously end up paying a major price for it in the end. In order to invest at the highest level, you need to do your research and make sure you have as much data as possible. When you do, you are mitigating risk and increasing your chances of success. The stock market can be quite intimidating; however, it does not have to be that way. Once you understand how it actually works, the biggest question you will have is: Why didn't I start sooner?

As you went through the chapters of this book, my hope is that you have a fundamental understanding of the stock market, including how to research and purchase the stocks you want. I went over some of the best platforms to begin your stock trading journey and also some of the techniques used by the best in the industry. This includes Warren Buffett, who is considered by many to be the greatest stock market investor of all time. As we rounded out the book, I went over some simple methods to create passive income in the stock market. Lastly, I discussed the benefits of value stocks and how they work.

One thing I don't discuss in this book is specific stock recommendations. That was not my objective here. I simply wanted to give you the tools to help you choose the best stocks for yourself. No matter how experienced, a stock investor is, you never want to go solely off their tips on which stocks to invest in. You must still do your own research to get the best long-term results.

You will continue to gain a better understanding of how the market works, as well, which is essential.

The next step is to take the information I went over in this book and start applying it in the real world. Once you are ready, which I hope is now, start looking at the platforms you want to use to start trading. Raise capital if you need to and also begin researching various stocks that you want to buy. Try focusing on value investing by paying attention to what the specific companies are doing, rather than the actual market. Once you have educated yourself, it's time to take a leap of faith and jump in. After all, even after thorough research, training, and experience, luck will always play a role to a certain degree. There will always be risks involved, but if you play your cards well, your winners will offset the losers, and you will end up with major gains in the end.

The more people that become aware of the information provided, the more individuals I am able to help. Therefore, if you enjoyed this book, please let me know your thoughts by leaving a short review on amazon. I want to thank you once again for reading it, and I hope it provided you with all of the valuable information you need. Now, let's go start creating some wealth in the stock market, like millions of others around the world.

CPSIA information can be obtained
at www.ICGtesting.com
Printed in the USA
BVHW040710220321
603170BV00004B/674

9 781801 535489